Black Swan

Elizabeth Martina Bishop

This book is dedicated to my maternal grandfather,

Charles DeWolfe Gibson

© 2013, Elizabeth Martina Bishop

Elizabeth Martina Bishop, Ph.D.
2675 West State Route 89A, #1100
Sedona, AZ 86336, USA

ISBN-13: 978-1491036433
ISBN-10: 1491036435

BISAC: Poetry / General

Design by Artline Graphics, Sedona
www.artline-graphics.com

Black Swan

Elizabeth Martina Bishop

TABLE OF CONTENTS

PART 1
Writing Class

PART 2
Momentary Embrace

PART 3
Publican's Half Story

PART 4
Burning the Body

PART 1

Writing Class

Fire Water

At the Black Swan Hotel, why did you dunk dark chunks of bread in watered-down wine?

Was there a return on your investment? Was there a ritual sense in anything you did? Did I miss something?

People let their lives play out in whatever challenges they have chosen to surmount. Remember how you always let us play charades? Pantomime games? But, O to find that sacred ground where all of the actors are silent.

Sacred Reruns

Rather than go fishing, some people prefer to watch reruns of their escapades. In that event, they begin over-singing the praises of everyone listed in the movie credits.

When frozen fists of embryos are detected in the womb from the first, no one knows the exact nature of the sacred script. But is it really sacred? Someone somewhere is bound to slip up.

As it is, knowledge of Odette or Odile is needed to understand human motivation and agenda.

Odette, Odile

Clothed in a black cloak, Michael Robartes waves a black wand. Everything that happens in life doesn't need to turn out right.

When Odette appears as Odile, She fools the prince and almost everyone in the audience. Suddenly, the conductor of the orchestra plays a key note everyone knows.

Michael Robartes would never wash his hands of swan feathers. Rather, he would build a soul moat on an island and let everyone worship but himself who had no thoroughfare for faith. One hand does not know what the other is doing. We make soul excuses for our misdeeds.

Loralie have always lured inveigled sailors to their death. Perhaps, now it is payback time. Yet, maybe the payoff is not worth the frailty of human life. Only in a harem's cradle, does one soul learn to crawl off in a corner and wonder about the history of prayer.

Ceremony

While dancing in wild abandon, a stampede grows in ocean's underbelly of avalanche that, churning, finally crescendos.

A procession of light follows of which each horse and statue is a part and parcel of a story. The height of waves in a measured spleen of shadow rising and falling.

The sea has perfected the life of the soul. Moon crescents are harbored in her womb. Until an ancient tide reconfigures itself, what are we doing living here on Mother Earth?

Prayer

And what of the men and women praying on the shore? Are you the only one holding a child on the feast day and ceremony honoring the four Marys? Haven't you ever heard the story before?

How the four Marys ever arrived on these shores remains a bit of a mystery. Scholars will not decide which legend must prevail. A gypsy woman offers a continual spate of prayers for the churching of her child as well as the purification of her body.

Suddenly, a photographer appears out of nowhere and discreetly snaps an irreverent picture. When she shouts at him, he spits in the direction of her skirt.

Camera Obscura

Saying he represented a glossy, new age magazine, the photographer insisted on another photo op. In a raucous voice, he remarked: the charlatans have let loose. How beautiful!

At last, a real piece of art! The miracle of his wide-angled lens has captured history in its prime. (That's what the photographer thinks.) What if your sister was praying and wanted privacy right then? A sacerdotal guerdon morphs into a possible occasion of revenge. She won't become a sacrificial lamb.

As this is not an occasion of sin but a celebration of the Feast of the Blessed Virgin, what of her tiny bundle of rags? There's never even been a baptism, has there? As you well know, what happens next defines the nature of a primordial dream-time.

Womb of a Cloud

While praying, a song rose up within her,–
a song enlivening the glistening swells of
ocean lightening. Wind and rain in the womb
of a cloud.★

One moment, the whole world seemed
dressed in a blinding light. The next moment,
it seemed as if light had never been.

Love disappeared in a lightening flash. In a
calm room of ocean, now a salt-riven
undertow devours her sleeping child.

A churning of water. Water's flight into the
ethers. What of her life? Chaos. Abyss.
Miasma. Her life, as she had known it, would
never appear the same to her.

★ From a traditional Scottish folk song

Transparency

Today, the picture looks blurry and faded like a transparency.

But this is one she never holds up to light.

What if the child's dying in the womb of ocean were covered up in the waking deeds of prayers' tremulous crescendos?

Now as the story begins unraveling, observe how love's wayward threads begin to dwindle, thicken, then fray, almost sundering themselves into the thinnest lines imaginable.

What parallels infinity's mile?

Waves of Grief

Recall to mind a picture of the horse's body exploding into multiple fragments. Tell me the charioteer was misguided and misjudged distances.

If memory cradles emptiness in bas-relief, what memory of the bardo? Between two sisters? Between mother and child? Between words never convened in thought.? Between one incarnation and another's memory, thoughts, lines blotted out. Between people and the in-between spaces of their hidden conversation?

What of the soul's inner core? Within a jade-colored ocean of dissonances, at the last moment, do you know someone who chooses love above all else?

Walking on Water

Between continents, why witness the pale blue yards of broadcloth stretching between us? While telling one another the story of our losses, we walk across a viaduct. A sensation of floating ensues. No one knows the underpinnings of grief, where one life begins and another leaves off.

I never thought I'd send my children to dive for black pearls off the sea coast, but it's expected. Everyone learns to swim and dive for gold sovereigns and pearls, even before they've reached their teens. Why mention drowning? Mimicking sea mollusks and sea grasses, isn't there a special power every child possesses?

What force allows us to swim into water's deepest caverns? Even underwater, the human body remains luminous, transparent, a precious force for good.

Writing Class

Now she's fallen on. She's pregnant. At 41, it isn't exactly a burden and yet it is. She suffers from a case of nausea and jitters.

She divorced in Italy and fell in love in Ennistymon, a little too quickly, but there it is. Whatever happens happens. Remanded in the custody of this kind of happiness, what else is there?

Everything in life matters when the physical is less obvious. She describes her Cousin Bertha. A lover of turquoise necklaces and rain dances. She's sure the little one she is carrying is Cousin Bertha who only died last year.

Reincarnation

Thank God for metaphysics to balance things out! To clear up any paltry tiny discretions. Any unkindness that might have been lingering in the shadows.

One day, didn't she have a dream about her cousin? A body has been chosen. She feels blessed. She throws up a little.

When her teacher brings her vodka on a tray, she declines his generous offer. She looks away from him into the blinding sun's rays. She knows better. So does Father Healy. He knows so much better, so he does.

Revelation

Her writing class at the Black Swan. Sam's wife tells her to create a costume out of the back pages of The Irish Sentinel. She laughs. To disclose the reason why she has vertigo would be to betray the irresistible nature of the sailor.

He visited Naples on her birthday last October. Details. Prenuptial agreements. Such a shyster. Heathen that he was. Unknown at the time, a man fallen prey to lower-chakra vices.

Somehow she feels compelled to review the details of her perilous and purblind tryst. She would now write a traditional poem based on a Provencal line-break. She conjured up pictures of make-believe flames flickering on shiny brown logs.

Interwoven with a host of Celtic dragons, soon to be emptied of its ashes, the hearth lay still and calm. Until the members of her class became entranced with the details of her half-story, she was never satisfied.

Seven Years Later

It is now seven years later and I am in this place facing all of you all over again.

Clueless, the girl remembers the beginning and end of a feckless affair.

The members of her class, do they remember the details of her story?

Soul poetry. Poetry slam. Poetry is a mere dalliance. Soul anguish. Soul romance. Soul radiance a mere dalliance.

At this point, the less said, the better.

How could she have imagined she'd ever been pregnant?

Or that the rug had been pulled out from under her?

PART 2

Momentary Embrace

Visitor's Book

What equals a sea-eagle's lament? Ocean's swells? It is easy stand still and leave no trace. What of the memory of a wave?

O seer's tongue, you're in an endless state of transition. Where is the blessing of grace?

In the crypt where our last meeting took place, near St. Wynnefred's Well, nothing had really changed.

I watched you as you gingerly entered your name in the visitor's book. Here were little messages left for the invisible eyes of saints and rowdy tourists to read at their leisure. Your entry read like the pages of an unwritten movie script:

You don't know anything of my story. Let the wind blow false accusations off the face of the earth. Past delicate lace work. Those billowing curtains from Normandy. I know what I know. I can't turn back the clock.

.

Sacrilege

When I met you in the recovery room, I discovered where we might have met before. Wasn't it true you had served as a mercenary among unknown flotillas of nurses at the Norwegian front during the war? Later, when I met you in the vestibule, I knew it was all over. Things between us had stalled.

While our meetings continued, they had this clandestine nature that keep us going full tilt.

So I continued. What of it? When I placed a wreath of flowers on the Madonna's head, why did I do this? I hadn't a clue? Fear? It seemed a natural thing to do. I mean to continue as we did.

Whatever the case, nothing seemed an act of sacrilege, not really. That which is forbidden should later be forgiven. Otherwise, the perpetrator remains anonymous and blank?

For a fortnight afterward, I remained somewhat chastened by our unchaste actions.

If not sooner or later, I know what would happen. I would begin wandering the streets at night looking for the bright lights of the heathen members of the gentry.

Deja Vu

When Sam told me he knew Ninette de Valois in a past life, that too seemed another act of sacrilege. How could I remind him of anyone? I'd never even met her. How would I know the difference?

He told me the gatehouse was under new management. It had been made into a glass factory. He wasn't lying when he told me life flows on like a river. Landfills became gardens for disenfranchised souls and their deliverance. Who are the tourists who like to parade around sacred sites wearing bifocals and flip-flop shoes?

Later, these folks choose to leave offerings of popcorn at the altars of the people who invented it along with yucca-blossom-type shampoos.

Twin Flames

Hope the meat keeps 'til I get home. When I turned to you and you turned to me, I could not believe anyone would sleep through this part in the movie.

She said, I can't believe you're leaving for your honeymoon tomorrow. One twin listens by a hearth stone in Wales. Another twin picks up the trail in Italy

Who can keep track of the wind? Explain human foibles. Your cancer is still in remission, isn't that a blessing!

In such indecent fables of the human heart, the fox is left staring at the grapes.

Behold, yet another unhurried episode in the story of the twin flames, mosquito bites, and succulent fruit.

False Prophets

Born out of wedlock, false prophets began circulating ancient news. People everywhere around announced abundant fairy sightings at New Grange.

Among standing stones in County Tyrone, more sacred sites were found in less time than you could shake a lamb's tail.

Carved-cross slabs announced the hereafter created by antique guardians of stone-cromlechs.

At the same time, village inhabitants also suffered from chilblains. Do you know they had previously lived on sheep brains?

Later, they had to deal with sudden incursions by cross-eyed Viking warriors. At the funeral, my cousin wouldn't even look at me. She just stared past me.

Narrowing her eyes to tiny slits, her daughter stuck out her tongue. She wore a green dress. The last time I saw her, she was clog-dancing in a ceilidhe held in a pub near Sligeach Parish.

Life goes on, no matter what.

Tall Order

How will the earth
    perfect itself through you?
How could you
    let the child slip into the ocean?
How could you
    dream yourself into a cardboard box?

Emerging intact, why do you think you'd
end up in one piece without some fallout?
Isn't this the part of the story where the
camera runs out of film?

Must it be made clear to you that horses
with flared nostrils are still running neck and
neck? Will things be this way until the end of
time?

Is the part of the story in which a canvas
crowds out all the other artists? As it is, how
can life with all its unique birds remain
undefiled, even purified?

Art Exhibit

I must tell you at the age of 77 years and four days, an old woman had her first art exhibition. Held in a local courthouse exhibition without fanfare, the exhibit featured familial art renditions of various animals and flowers.

Only blind people were invited to come forward and touch the rough-hewn texture of the pleasant canvases.

After this fact was revealed by someone operating under unimaginable conditions of anonymity, other details later emerged vis a vis anonymous bystanders who attended the art opening in full regalia.

Meanwhile who can remain unmoved when rumors fly through Braille fingers of the moon?

Foxes in the Park

By the way, what of those foxes in the
park? What are their chances of survival?
Their presence assured a day replete with
issues of estrangement and malaise. The
implications of disintegration of the rose.

During the long hot summer afternoons, I
felt you could begin to understand. Mirrored
in self-defeating patterns, how could you be
blinded by another's self-pity?

I touch your hand.
Sweet sadness.

Yet, on some level,
love may never have existed.

Daubs of Paint

During that long afternoon we spent together, you knew a pregnancy might ensue. You took a chance, didn't you?

A daub of paint on the wall reminds me of the blank bleak walls at the Kensington Hotel.

That which you perceive as truth is never what is fully meant. I decided to carry the child. The executioner's noose was in place.

Blackbirds sing about the terms of a conventional marriage. Never mentioned in subsequent issues of Bird Song Warbler News, the details of the Cesarean birth.

Gabriel

Like a serpent staring at all kinds of women, Gabriel, what has become of you? Our meeting was for half-past eleven.

Gabriel, why do you avoid me? Why do you absent yourself from the labyrinth of life? Though I'm wearing pink high heel shoes, this happens every time we meet. Once again you have dishonored me.

Is it true she said: I will lose you somehow in this crowd of well-wishers? In this mystic sea of transfigured oceans, you'll never miss my going. Gabriel, I promise you, I will never be your wife.

I will live alone and enjoy my solitary life.

New Forest

At what cost, that old adage that applies to you so well: You do not know how to follow anyone, not even your own kinsfolk and family.

Thus, among gypsy fairs, you're found wandering,– eternally wandering, a streeler, and a mumper. As a wayfaring traveler, I know you're not looking for me. So what does it matter?

Let me tell you this. You will never find me. I'm good at hiding. Isn't it true what they tell me: that the other woman has made her bed in your house? With her three children are camped in your back yard as permanent fixtures, what do you expect?

Let bygones be bygones. Let's build an addition to our back porch before we become some kind of strangers to ourselves.

Gypsy

Another woman sees me at the fair. She's less than discreet when she asks: whatever became of that traveler,– whatever-his-name-is? They know you are a gypsy, Gabriel. Everyone is after you.

I thought it dangerous to even picture you in the way I did. If you're living in a bender-tent under someone else's shadow in fits and starts, why bother to show off your hot-tempered horse-coper's wits?

Nevertheless, since everyone knows the truth about you, I'll give them this.

It's more than once you've combed my hair.

Exile

What were you doing in the Black Swan Hotel, Gabriel?

At the root of all your dreaming spells, a spate of robberies deferred. Why else could you do but remain in exile from more than one city at a time?

As it is, you already live in a broken-down world of half-truths and misspent lies. Even if angels have all but abandoned you, why do you keep running back to me?

Forgive me, but perhaps, I am more famous for running off infrequently with more than one jazz musician.

Logic

What is the logic of the Black Swan?

Why is it you never mastered any chords on the mandolin?

At a time like this, you need to do something to cover for your deficits.

What demon has me going back and forth,– sometimes with you, sometimes without. I'm half of a mind to let you go, Gabriel.

You've drunk up all the vodka in the room. I was saving it for those odd occasions when, without letting me know anything, you'd would walk away from me and disappear into the mist.

UFO Landing

Check out The Daily News for various editions of extraterrestrial landing sites. What's available to you in a city near you?

For you are haunted by a vision of yourself, reconfigured as the muse. And yet, aren't you quite the charlatan and handyman by trade?

Whenever you comb my hair, Gabriel, you lean into the sullen blue embers of the North Star. If my life counts for nothing, what of your life?

You know what? Your life exists only for me, Gabriel. For no one else. Your sense of the theatrical is only meant for me. You're quite the man.

I've heard you muttering under your breath. Did you hear me correctly when I said what I said countless times? Which one of us would pass first?

Are you deaf like the rest of them I've half-heartedly wedded and bedded down?

One day, I'll leave you, Gabriel, so I will. I promised my higher self. My soul contract is lying over there on Emily Dickinson's shelf.

I'm Leaving You

What did you mean when I said to you: I will unpeel you from my retinue of servants? Why did you stand there as mute as a parrot, a parakeet on lock-down in a brass cage?

Seems like you are a gypsy without a destiny. Whatever the case, I know I'm in way over my head. Try imposing a curfew on love's vainglorious deeds.

I know I can go on torturing myself with my suspicions about your other lovers, but still... I dream of not following you. What good does it do? We've been living in the same box-car for three years.

Other Woman

In another body, I could have been with you quite differently.

Drawing on my shamanic imagination, I begin rebuilding your form in reconfigured ice-pillars. Beneath your still more colder hands, I grow older.

I'm even more confused and forlorn than when I began meeting you.

Gabriel, don't tell me what the other woman did to you, nor you to her.

I pity your lame excuses.

I don't want to hear another word.

Imposter

An impostor among absurd humming-
birds,– aren't you the excellent provider
you've said you were?

Or, once again, are you lying through your
teeth? Flying on invisible high-wires? How
many times have your tangled soul chords
begun to pull apart?

Once more I find myself mystified by the
curious turning of knobbed roots. Gnarled
branches seem to spell disaster for me as well
as for others.

Other dancers you've recently picked up,
they would concur with me, would they not?
Don't tell me Sue drank bourbon in the park.
However brief her sad story, I want no part in
her self-pity.

Why does the other woman always linger
in the wings?

Reunion

Let's get back together. Let's do the rabbit dance like we used to do.

You know I'll never leave you, Gabriel. Everything will be all right, won't it? I'm the only one who owns your wicked heart. Doesn't that count for anything?

I'm on my knees to you. I grieved our parting even before our meeting near a beauty parlor on the Adriatic coast.

How quickly I forgot Count Oppersdorf!

Moonlight

The meaning of this dream will eventually come clear: the necklace, the negligee, the scarf. As an Empress card, she could not have been more dangerous than she was. In fact, she pulled the worst card in the deck. Weren't there other cards she could have drawn?

What was she to do? She couldn't hide the meaning of the card from him. Where was it she'd heard the maxim: No man is an island? How true this was!

All she wanted to do was to crawl back into her dungeon's turret's tower and let down her hair.

.

Trust

We need to learn to try and trust one another. What I mean is this. If I trusted you right now, maybe we'd both end up sleeping under a bridge or two.

We could do well enough to live on bramble and nettle tea. We wouldn't clog our arteries doing that, now would we?

Maybe tomorrow night, we'll get it right and break the curse of inclement weather.

Yet if I revealed what I truly thought, I believe my soul might fly away for good.

Moon Craters

The glass in your hand, the blue contours of the glass. Your reflection haunts me in my dreams.

The lights around you. What is their meaning in Aramaic? Demons or angels?

Will the Emerald Tablets set me free upon a harmonious course of action in which my path is judicially set?

Moonlight has never imagined itself into such lurid postures as these. Though we're somewhat self-assured in our birthright, please.

The last man who was to have visited the distant reaches of the moon-craters, who was he really?

I never tired of seeing him curled up in the corner of my living room.

Birth and death are as final as the wings of life in the soul's sanctimonious journey of him who is indifferent to the taste of brambles on the tongue.

How could love go wrong? The longer we live the greater the chances to miscalculate the ease at which a beast swallows a wagon.

PART 3

Publican's Half Story

Shaker Village

There is error in the meaning of words.

This man will not take a chance on end-stopped lines nor chants recited in villages of rhyme.

For whatever she's worth, this woman will not take trouble to do anything but pick fruit of a wine-filled orchard or turn butter in the churn. Neither will she note the angle of the sun as it casts a shadow on her plantation pock-marked by overgrown weeds.

At least, there is an insignia of the Tree of Life embedded in the straight back chairs she has designed. There is error in the meaning of words. Within the world of speech, nothing is properly defined.

Sometimes stones will not move nor speak of the bitter bread of love and love defiled by open ended caesuras.

Contrary to all accounts, we were not moved by reports pertaining to the taste of wine and the bittersweet nectar on our tongues. Unmoved by the taste of water, the taste of wine, the widow of timeless time failed to halt in her tracks.

Nothing within could beseech her to summon her guardian angels. Such angels were no longer convinced of their existence either.

True, though she studied scripture every day and made journal entries, once she began to spin on a mahogany floor, you'd never know the end or the beginning of her story.

Once turning on her heels to sway, to spin, to sing before the tintinnabulation of the piano keys, the shadows ended as her body began to vanish.

And yet there was proof of her existence. Wasn't it true she made entries about casualties of the French and Indian wars? Didn't she write about birch bark heroes pretenders to the throne of Tecumseh's pagan bones?

If trees were curling constantly inwardly on themselves instead of outwardly dwelling, the visible architecture measured in mahogany timbers and rafters, then you can figure on something viable that existed in her life.

There is error in the meaning of words frozen this child will not live but plunge her hands into well water to remember the memory of what breath had been for just a season she had lived.

In that time of war that child will escape an incarnation return to begging in a neighborhood where in laws bivouac and hidden hearths.

There is error in the meaning of words for the bleached bones of elders turned to ash. The kingdom of omens and mirror remained unblemished in Kentucky forests and woods.

If we die of the darkness and not cold, who remembers if we live even after that?

Artist

Unhurried, unperfected, unaware of how unearned tax credits could impair or harm the previous occupant of his tweed jacket, he patiently awaited final sentencing at his trial.

He wanted to offer a toast to all those who typically preferred to avoid the scurrilous and scandalous messages of nightingales.

In the name of daffodils, azaleas, and laurel he wondered which chakra would offer him a platform for his bird-song trilogies.

Still, he remained unaware his tweed coat was in fact a sinecure of the one he used to wear in Paris at all the art openings he'd attended.

Job Security

In fact, he wanted his body to keep on flowing in the same way, in a world peopled with fields of marigolds, in a world overrun by a series of people all saying the same thing.

Yet, caught in the spokes of unhurried wisdom, the Wheel of Fortune card gave him a quiet jolt to his psyche.

He was not sure of the world to which he belonged perhaps he belonged. Perhaps to a different trade union run by sailors not tailors and tweed weavers.

He felt Buddha's brows bearing down on him. For the Buddha born without an eye was as unfamiliar to him as the grackle is to me.

Under hypnosis, however, he admitted he had aspirations that had remained hidden more of his waking life.

Not as a minimalist painter. Not as a mountebank without a herd of wild animals. Not as a jailer with a turnkey.

Perhaps he'd may have unbecome himself becoming another edition of himself at a later date.

Waiting by a River

I wait. I am the river. I grow. I am free. I am the spirit of the pine-tree expanding, ever expanding.

I have been waiting 14 years. I look at the clouds and stitch blue threads that wound the green-eyed foxes crouching in the forest.

Eyes are not here. I am threads of water opening. I no longer know who I am. Do you know? Have you heard me?

Am I heard? Why deny me?

I am no longer the answer within this blood, nor the bones of the body misunderstood. Water knows what is good.

I want to be all the words you might have said. I want to be words without speaking about any of them.

I want to be the leaves inside the leaves. I want to dance inside a cage of canaries in emotions misperceived and displaced.

You insist your relatives are of John Wesley's ilk. This in itself carries memories.

Lyons

I'd like to explain to you how I met my husband. I'm not sure where he came from originally. Perhaps from a Lyons orphanage run by the Sisters of Mary?

I know one thing, though. I always carry a Bible under my arm for my protection and safe-keeping. I can't forget what a poet my husband was before I met him.

When he was began dating me he dedicated several poems to me. Today, I'm old hat to him,– rather unimportant. Now he's tongue-tied,– like everyone else, he appears nothing extraordinary.

Yes, they call me Marie. How did you know? His name is Albert.

Beautifully scripted as the fragile rain that confesses an embrace extending to cedar and cypress trees. Of course, all the things he spoke about so eloquently were incapable of ever being adequately translated.

We left our homeland for reasons of financial constraint. At the time, I carried one pamphlet with me that put forward this important question: do you know where the tower of Babel is located?

Marie zeroes in on her pamphlet and tries to answer her own question. I'm so glad you asked. So many have closed the door on me because of who I am. Although I am spotless before the eyes of God, there is one thing I fear.

Those crazy looking deer, what do you call them in your language? Mule deer? A moose, my dear, a moose, my dear. That's what made you choke on your burrito this morning.

Logger's Camp

For years, he's camped out, living on elderberry wine and free handouts from men who pity those who live in homeless shelters.

Whenever he played the guitar, he thought he'd reincarnated with the spirit of John Lennon. He wasn't quite sure. Some spirit, though, of some celebrated person took him over. That's what made his riffs so dangerous.

Last summer, didn't he heed the voice of the wind? As he approached Tamarisk Mountain, his ears began to twitch. Still, he was afraid to camp out on the back porch where card-players in bedroom slippers couldn't decide what to do about escaped convicts.

Bounty

Save his pelt? How much was he worth? He waited for turtles and foxes to bring him messages.

They never did. He refused to drop the mask. Without a driver's license, who would he become? Would People for the Ethical Treatment of Animals seek to coax from him a string of beaver trapped easily in a season of reruns? Would they want compensation for incursions into the wilderness?

Ah, what a lovely mink coat you're wearing this year. My dear, you look simply gorgeous.

Winner take all? Avoiding bagging, drugging, sedating.

More than mystery play plot lines are needed to defray the cost of salvation's loss in Playback Theatre's theatrical antics on back porches.

Fur Trapper

Animals must run free. Trappers need to act responsibly.

Until rendered half-comatose, beneath a surgeon's scalpel, who could foresee a bobcat's destiny or a poacher's dream go up in smoke?

While wavering between this life and the next, what ever happens, happens.

While the ghosts of shorter poems continue harboring presentments, can one consider the run-off of a broth worth cooking on an open fire?

About Her

I had two dreams about her.

First Dream

What do you want to know?

The first dream was the one she claimed, she would never forget. Did you want to tell her poems stem from a place of peace and no where else?

Platforms and docks where people dry their clothes after jumping in rivers, ponds, and various bodies of water. That's what poetry heralded. Unshepherded herds wandered out of reach. They existed only for those who never entertained any dreaming thoughts at night.

Second Dream

She was dancing. What do you mean: she was dancing? With whom? I mean, her dress exploded like a cornhusk ripening in autumn filled with amber and marigold colors.

And you know what was happening in that field? The last time I caught sight of her, she was spinning and still dancing in a Festival of Life.

During the day you couldn't discern the

noisy festivities. All you could hear is the rattling of china on the mantle.

Neither could you help from hearing the rustling of branches in wind's mockery of betrayal.

Woven into wreaths for her auburn hair almost nightly the dreams appeared as deer limping towards water troughs.

Nothing more than that.

Colonel's Dream

They say he was a colonel who was a lover of impressionist paintings. Marigolds were his favorite flowers. At least that's what she believed he said. In fact, no one would dispute that.

The one thing that still eluded him, however, was vanquishing his fear of death that was still proved overwhelming.

How can he prove something were true if you've never opened a wine bottle on a picnic table covered with a cloth? How could he broker army boots? His past was a make-believe palace of wounds. How could you resuscitate the dream?

It seems you arrived relatively unscathed in wartime. Now, it's the same thing all over again. What made your memory of life so fearful, so terrifying? You broke an egg you found in a bird's nest when you were nine

Nostalgia

You mean you never played the trombone beore we met? I thought you said you were a regular on American Idol.

As a sign of better things to come, you mean you didn't meditate on a hummingbird resting on a trumpet vine or honeysuckle?

Though your dark mouth boasts the privilege of words framed in unlettered oaths, you mean you never served in the foxholes of Vietnam?

You mean you don't hold the keys of your existence? You mean you've often indiscriminately welcomed ghosts into your den and your living room and never even batted an eyelash when light-bulbs exploded?

You mean you watched the old hag dialogue with the ex-marine who had been shot through the back of the neck?

They had perfect word recognition through harmonious telepathic exchanges. Though he was still alive, he was mute. He couldn't speak.

Life is like that, isn't it? I can't make head nor tail of it, can you?

That's why I remain a recluse.

Approaching Lamy

We were on the train heading through Lamy. Tiny drops of rain hit snow hedges along the way. Your face across a table now.

The waitress has permitted it. We don't have to sit side by side like two pigeons on a telephone wire, two pigeons on a railing. Our hair is falling long across the table.

The waitress, a lioness pauses to purr. Like Isis, or a member of a mystery school, she seats two other passengers across from us.

Mother and daughter. They look totally out of place. Why do they choose the railway dining car as a sparring match between lioness and cub?

The waitress offers them a menu. They have chosen light buttered toast and tea. The waitress is trying to hold the world in one steady gaze.

Tiny snowdrops are poking through Mother Earth next to dried up rivers.

No one will want to hold water jars on their heads on a day like this.

Journal Entry

I

One of the last entry she wrote in her notebook two weeks before she died said: I want you to remember, I am your daughter, no matter what.

Even if I have to cross the silence that leaps between us like flames. I feel like every time I talk to you, I have to introduce myself as someone new.

II

The last entry the daughter put in her diary was: I never loved my husband I always hated him. Even though we have only been married two months, I wonder why life has the power to inspire us to take unnecessary actions? I've been in a bad mood ever since I married.

III

Another entry my daughter made in her clandestine journal: The other girl, the Greek in the quartet keeps throwing herself on my husband. You call love an infatuation?

Now, that I am an old married woman, I wonder if that's really true. Of course, we're surrounded by the trappings of music in other small cabaret orchestras.

Clarinets, flutes, trombones – whatever you want, you name it, music is still music.

IV

Another mysterious entry:

I've been running my exercise tape over and over and over. I've been thinking of losing weight.

As luminous moonlight falls gently through the window, we'll never get it straight what we meant to one another.

Should I forsake death in the context of loveless marriage?

Mom, please don't read my diary. At least not right away. Wait awhile, ok?

Midnight

Unmet the midnight of my body, my body lacks a roof. A floor, a wall, a walkabout. My body lacks a boarding house of sparks. Sparks that fly up before the mansion of the wind.

My body lacks a mind that can swallow the mind of itself. You know where the villages are. You know what the town is. Almost as a consequence of nothing else, adobe structures spring up everywhere.

But you'd stop short of calling on foxes to devour the vestigial remains of bodies left after cranes set upon them. Nothing has been left in the garden. Fences are left untended Stone statues are left unguarded and eyeless.

Your life was a galaxy. You cared more for art than men or women. Dogs or children.

You cared more for god than angels. Now the water jar has exploded, it couldn't hold water because card-carrying sheiks on camels made you burn inside your robes with unexplained mystery of homeless paupers.

The water jar has exploded because the bones of water could not hold the sparks of love nor the majesty of light emanating nor the clay voice of the dead already dead to the world. Because the bones of water couldn't hold leaves, the tongues of man the form of a servant.

The soothsaying of a clairvoyant who knew the logic of madness had not ended her life. Birds are not crying. Friends are no longer devoted. No one reads my poetry.

You move, you rest, you follow the road. You spar with place as if there were nowhere. As if there were no moon to seize, no parcel of blame to appoint, you rise in the company of owls sitting on rooftops in forests of midnight owls who hold the compass of crying wind that stun and spin and amaze.

Who will understand why the owl trembles in your stumbled sleep, a troubadour of sound come back to your senses once and for all.

The dispossessed jewels of a cactus, the ocean of love are arraigned and argued in a court of law.

I am the one who reads the script. I am the one who readies it for consumption.

Who will recover the dead body and assign it to law-abiding citizens?

Until further notice, I am no longer assigned to initiates. It's only that I have lingered longer than is necessary in this life.

Let love prevail!

Treasure

Though we horde the spoils of battle, we don't want to share them with anyone.

While believers know where the gold is, a crowd of heathens have already pawned it to feather their nests.

We've recorded messages and we've heard all day from mourning doves and mayors of electoral offices in cities and towns.

We know where the gold is but we shy away from comets coming into their own luminance among intergalactic eons. We know where the treasure is and yet we've become blessed with aubades, ballads, and charades, garden enclosures that spring up in palisades every day.

We've become enamored of princes who hold the keys to change. They themselves won't change. We've painted masks on crocodiles so they only appear to savor meat floating in rivers.

While such rivers flow through beleaguered provinces, the guilty one addresses issues of love. At the cost of what mistake? A snowflake comes twirling falling in love's chandelier of fire.

How beautiful the woman's hairpiece. But it is counterfeit passed around among friends and purged of live energy.

We must confide in one another. We must turn the world upside down looking for buried treasure as foxes. Like demons kick over the traces of carrion they have fed on for years Yet a stone melting in the ground never really melts at all.

The astrologer consults his oracle of numbers, repeats messages. Only then does he dream he is a comet in a casket.

The soul's inventory has collapsed. The money system has collapsed. Turn loose the dog in a field of daisies or in a field of marigolds.

Where can he find peace? In the wilderness?

Pilgrimage

We'll start out smiling on our journey.

We know nothing of the companions along the way. We know nothing of the city of our limbs, whether they will give out or sing or become paralyzed.

You have purchased a young pup to stave off death. While yearning for a new life, dark shadows assail your debt to the mansions of the self.

One evening, when you invite a friend over for dinner, you feast on goose. The wishbone, the meat, falls off the bone all to easily. You comment to your friend: The wings have become extinct. You ask her "Which of the dogs will be burned, the young pup or the old dog?"

How do you start the journey not knowing anything of how things will turn out? Not knowing if the flower will burn perfectly in the desert. Not knowing if you'll come upon the truth. Not knowing no one wants to walk in your shoes or to interpret metaphors.

They want to claim all the dreaming for themselves or, for the dreaming to be done for them by someone else. If a person is dying of cancer, they want donations for research.

Not flowers. Not flowers perching on a landscape of the soul.

We'll start out smiling on this journey.

How the journey will end is anyone's guess. That's where ashes come in funerary urns and cameramen take close-ups of people in the throws of death.

Agoraphobia

Who lives in this house of dreams?

I'm not sure how many ghosts are napping in stone sepulchers, in parachutes. Who lives here? I'm not sure at all. But I'm sticking with an uncertainty principle.

Time synapses mapped. I've been caught napping for a long time. If blue wolves enter this sacred place, they interrupt, they intrude upon my heart-space. They come looking for carrion, for bones, anything that ferial cats would look for would do them proud.

This poem resembles no other I've written. That's why I've put down taproots among weeds. That's why I say it is absurd to go out to assume anything about wind driven autumn leaves.

The wind makes me restless. Her husband dove into cement. He can't come back. Now, how can I get out of that? his wife said to me.

The wind makes me restless. This woman lost a child. How can I get out of that? A thief burying a knife, stares blankly at his prey. I don't want to belong as long as this poem comes over me. Sings to me in the Siberian Tundra.

They were talking about catching a bear.

The interpreter said to the hunter, put your hands up over your head.

In the inaction of the syllable, there rests a hive of unsuspecting bees.

Skipping Stones

I

Poems for skipping stones. She used to sing poems about skipping stones. Lakes were textured like glass where whispered half-moons from her finger tips slid beneath the salmon paths.

She used to sing while she skipped stones the stones leapt from the water. She used to sleep by the water during the winter where she sang into the green flames of frozen fires.

II

The name of the most holy angels. The crimson cold blood stilled within the stilted bone made fables out of swans. Made the eyeless mole divide tunnels. She used to sing over skipping stones and against the welter of words. The waterfalls of time that wounded her.

III

She used to skip stones while coins hung from her lopped earlobes that defined her. Undercover she sang the nostalgic songs of love.

The notes however did not last. Soon she was exile by a history of sparrows that defined her hands. She used to sing into the plucked

broken strings of lyre and to the strings of a
harp stolen by princes of the wind.

IV

Her mind minted by the coinage of gold
music she drew from over the cypress trees on
the mountain. These songs slaved her in a song
of secrecy. Where was she from? Was she from
the silver bearing caves from Sacramento in
Granada?

V

She used to sing over cricket and gnat
infested water, until her hair silvered with
water she echoed the curses that were give to
her—she and sang from the tips of her shoes
banging across her heels.

VI

Under the curse of wild birches she knew
the silver fox could interpret her footsteps and
those of the departed ghost. Hers was the
harvest of journeys wedded on the stone of
knife-grinders.

She used to sing over skipping stones, and
shout over mirrors of glass. Let me pass.

What You Never Said

I

It would be wrong to say the harpist
moved on, passed on, took a new body.
Moved upstairs, went camping, or visited. The
neighbors. When he was in the hospital, his
mother said he moved away. It was at that time
he began watching a long movie.

II

There's a picture of him as a child with
fluffy blond curls. Balanced on a huge rock, he
looks like one of the ant people who crawled
on mother earth in this time and this place.

III

It would be wrong to choke back the
laughter of mentors, mendicants, spirit guides,
it would be too much. Life would have lost its
purpose to explain how he got away. The
words of the song he sang varied with a
landscape and firmament that was voracious
and pregnant with a force more powerful than
death.

IV

It would be wrong to say he merged with
an eagle And he continued on the track of
several wanderers who enjoyed riding in box
cars Birds hanging out in cactus-like apparatus
Inventive birdhouses

V

It would be wrong to say looking at the voice of the bride of light we learn to live in this chosen world of omens where we experience flight as painful as the preparation for anchoring birth.

VI

It would be wrong to say his entire life Served as a preparation for his ungainly disappearance. Wrong to say ocean demystify the person of the harpist. Our bodies are fashioned of whale bone and a silky green water and the smoke linked to an umbilicus.

It would be wrong to say that he visited the nighthawk. That he was unable to merge with a bevy of pigeons

VII

It would be wrong to say the words he spent in time's blessing were misspent and could not echo a sense of belonging.

It would be wrong to say he wrung his spirit clothes Out to dry, to say that his speech became an impediment to love that he was one of two sons I had one conspiratorial, one not so.

VIII

It would be wrong to say it was because the moon was in Capricorn He lost touch with his pen pals among hurdy-gurdy players Castanet players and bone dice players

IX

It would be wrong to say such is the soul
that it goes on jaywalking for those in love
exuding elegance in a divination of all that
grows in lush grass that will not drift away.

X

It would be wrong to say he opened doors
and windows and transfigured God's radiant
majesty in all, he did not say.

Hypnotic Regression

I

We were talking about hypnotic regression. In lieu of any reincarnation issues, what this could mean to Charles was truly devastating. As Charles was putting on his tweed coat to go out hunting, and replay a stag hunting expedition, while Charles was holding a book entitled Shoot if you must.

II

He started letting book titles get ahead of him He said, it's not my fault I was such an avid hunter from the moment I could walk I blessed the silence between me and my relatives I was transfixed by the beauty of innocent flames.

III

Meanwhile, I tell myself I must be dreaming. Why would I want to go stag hunting all over again? Meanwhile I am drowning under the weight of thousands of words medical researchers have been called in to reassure me of the heartbeats of broken birds who have migrated out of season.

IV

Yes, that's right we were talking about
hypnotic regression It starts with a countdown
and a confusion and a meltdown conceding to
the surrender pertaining to previous lives.

It starts with a lawyer and how he was not
in love with his wife Instead he was in love
with Europe It starts with a confusion May
you recognize in this life the sacred presence
of the divine.

V

Do not become addicted to a ghost. A man
who was lost and your coworker beyond a
theatrical facade. She said, I am in touch with
Chris, the man of the moment. A moth is
ambushed by the innocent flames of light.
Can't I remove the veil? The workshop leader
said I no longer love my husband so I
continue to regress and regress, further and
further away from the light.

PART 4

Burning the Body

Landing Strip

When I visited the Louvre, I noticed a picture hanging on the wall. It was The Last Supper fashioned in delicately-woven beadwork.

Perhaps it had been donated by the Mohawk Indians from around the Syracuse region of upstate New York. Truly, I'd never seen such marvelous handiwork.

When I heard that the man who was to have accompanied me on my subsequent journey to Paris failed to possess so much as an electric blanket or a toaster, I was flabbergasted. Wasn't there a way to turn back the clock. Hadn't I canceled the details of our soul contract?

I seem caught in between worlds. Engendered by landing strips and esplanades, what if the artist's model was left embedded in the last letter of a cosmic Mayan alphabet?

Unable to extricate herself, would she become a hobo goddess or a hypothetical muse? Perhaps the members of The Hudson River School have always had the last word.

Art Walk

Unguessed, a lovely heliotrope bloomed lonely by an electric fence. As my assigned art companion in the museum tour accompanied me to an outdoor swimming pool, containing a miniature replica of a waterfall, he confessed an unadulterated adulation for safari treks and theme parks.

What had become of the other members of the hunting expedition? Where had they gone? Had some of them become victims of bygone eras during the gold rush or were they misplaced items on white-river rafting escapades?

Mohawk Prince

Encompassed as he was by the Adirondack mountains, he wondered to himself, was there any point in accompanying Sue on subsequent museum tours and art treks?

Everything seemed a bit forced and a bit off-course. Since Brad remained blissfully unaware, he wondered had he really been a Mohawk prince or not?

As he glanced at a bevy of curlews flying overhead, he decided to anchor love in a carefully constructed nest his other lover Marion built for him besides an empty building.

Ski Lodge

And yet, Brad was disinclined to accept Sue's invitation to a ski lodge during the winter months.

All in all, he told himself, this incarnation he had been going through had an uneasy feel to it.

Yes, as if I were trapped in a subterranean catacomb, always with the wrong woman.

With all those other mouths to feed, – nothing turned out quite the way I wanted, Brad admitted sheepishly.

Perspective

Among unlikely Bohemian mobs, an artist suddenly drew an unlikely rendition of certain untamed shadows.

In one sweep across the canvas, he told himself, you've got to do what you've got to do. If you're not Argüelles' cartographer, it's best not to describe which laws of perspective apply and do not apply.

If you're a heron standing on one leg, in a timeless map of history, know this, suddenly your shadow may be eclipsed.

When your shadow is devoured by too much or too little sunlight, it's possible your body may morph into a form reminiscent of hybrids fertilized by pollen-bearing honey bees.

What explorer would text message himself the following: Put away your astrolabe, your compass, the sextant in your pocket.

At that point, you may be able to retrieve the entire universe vis a vis digital's virtual reality. Out of context, a matrix within a matrix,– a house of falling leaves.

Columbus

Columbus needed a job. The ad in the paper sounded most alluring: Discover the New You. Come, be an artist's model in Amsterdam.

What had he to lose? Long ago, his mortgage had slipped into hands of loan sharks. His girlfriend had jumped ship.

A death mask or a terra cotta replica of what he was seemed all the same to him as much as the muse to poets drowned in love.

As moonlight shouted through window panes, Eric Satie continues composing Gymnopedie offstage.

One evening, the artist's model announced, "I want to purge the world of every possible visionary source of potential attachment. I wish to purify my body through a course of Reiki medicine."

At that moment, a small bird fell against the shutters of a window.

Role Reversal

As the artist's model looked at her, he wondered if she was still in love with him. Outside the window of the art school, her eyes wandered to a sylvan grove. Just look at those antlers on that moose, she cried.

Now the artist's model saw himself straddling two timelines. In one timeline, he was a giant moose in that sylvan glade. In another timeline, he felt he'd been downloaded as a miniature mule deer hunting for fodder. True, he hadn't too much going for him.

Suddenly, the artist model blurted out the truth, between you and me and flag pole, I don't understand anything about issues of abandonment.

I took this post because I needed additional pocket change. Sensing his unease, she gently probed, isn't there a better movie than this one you could star in?

When a wild rabbit finds itself ensnared in the warrens of a dilapidated movie set, what happens next?

Upon being offered a better opportunity, who accepts paid-per-view?

Mystery School

Or was the contractual nature of his love contained within a membrane of a turtle egg?

Or was love contained with a drunken cloud depicted in an empty sky?

Or did love move waltzing into the stone rooms of a melancholy moon?

Or was love confined within the practices of the ragged hedgerow schools celebrated during the reign of Henry VIII?

Or did love shine through stained glass windows?

Or did love move to contain the ragged spirit of silence?

She would never deign to explain exactly to which mystery school she belonged. Thus, she remained a ghost of his former self, scarcely worth talking to.

 Marigold

No matter how many times she had rehearsed this scene on movie sets, she remained confused. Foreclosure was just around the corner.

What was love really? Was love the nesting box of disorder to which he subscribed on a per-diem basis?

Was love her womanly body pinned to a bowsprit of a boat harbored in Arles? Was she Theo? Was he Vincent? Was Cezanne still Cezanne?

Was the man writing a guide to art exhibitions being fair to the man with the marigold-colored beard?

Nest

All her life it seemed to her, love appeared as the empty container for surreal metaphors?

What about an empty nest created by a flock of sparrows leaving a place where they so recklessly wintered? Should demolition squads be summoned? What of the strikes among meat packer's unions?

Considering the fascination one has about death, why waver over life's uneven cornices?

Why fracture mythologies based on uneasy mosaics?

Vertigo

Why are stories passed around?

Without wild drinking parties would life ever be the same? At such gatherings, someone always ends being maligned or carried out on a stretcher.

Whatever you do, please summon a union organizer a person who will ensure that artists are not excluded from the prize-giving committees.

While one artist goes out on a duck-shooting expedition, another one writes about his broken heart. Later, the third contestant undertakes critical analysis of a theatrical piece de resistance.

In this instance, I hesitate to lend credence to anything stated from anyone suffering from vertigo.

Not a drop has passed my lips, for that matter, did you catch sight of the multiple cracks in the mirror hanging in the hallway?

Vanishing Point

Why falsify the heart of love?

Mrs. Moonshine, haven't you worn the same piece of graying lace off the shoulder for centuries?

And yet, according to the laws of perspective, the hidden vanishing points, do they remain the same no matter in what lifetime they appear?

A British medium put a sign up in her window in bold letters:

Yes, I talk to dead people all the time.

The moment she put up that sign, a storm of feathers erupted among every single angel guarding angelic pathways and corridors.

At that moment, another sign was posted in the window:

Anyone found under drinking age will be drawn and quartered, perhaps even in an undisclosed location.

If anyone is caught drinking dandelion wine, even in infinitesimal amounts, you will never hear the end of the story.

Expect a plethora of New Age parking tickets and subsequent foreclosure notices disowned and thrown away.

Snow Melting on Sunlit Hills

Since her reading Phaedrus had been banned, she spent most of her time snapping photos of impossible situations.

She felt excluded from the birthday of the damned.

Who were they all, anyway? Unsavory Philistines?

Were they disciples or followers who reveled in the words of Aristophanes or not?

The Space Between Us

She wondered, should have she moved to Arles? Or to Thrace? Or to Crete? Or to Knossos? Or somewhere else?

How could she define herself according to the parabolas of astral cartography of time and space?

Especially, this seemed difficult when everything on earth appeared as a counterpoint to flaming comets.

Then, too, seaweed was banned and discarded. It certainly should not have been ingested by Siberian reindeer herds.

She was downloading images at such a pace. The author of the Life of Cézanne had himself gone made from syphilis, thus echoing the challenge of the life he was trying to recreate.

Several trips to the Russian Orthodox Church could not patch up the relative distance that persisted between himself and his doctor.

Reverie

So, what is the Buddha nature of the artist, really about?

Unorthodox, maverick, bohemian, the consummate charlatan with a dozen masks?

Should she pattern her life after a plaster cast of a sea mollusk? What about the death mask of the poet Keats? Should she rather align herself with the task of Aesop's Fables?

Was there any one image to which she could surrender? She had an innate fear of her love for fool's gold. Strange illusions confused her senses and make obstacles out of karmic debts.

A lotus grown in a garden of fire can never be manicured.

As a perfected seascape, a mirror of desire, all in all, was she a sea eagle or not?

Feast Day

What was this all about, Malvinia's ghost?

What a very old woman she'd seemed in this life.

An indolent gypsy explained that what had happened had occurred over one hundred years ago. She carried around a blurred picture of Malvinia.

How could she fall in love with a ghost? Love is blind. It wasn't her fault. What improvident wisdom accompanied her during the course of her entire life?

The blessing of water and small ships was about to take place in the harbor during St. Joseph's Feast Day.

Shuffling the Cards

In subsequent lifetimes, depending on which one you mean, everyone might admit God has the first and last laugh.

Only as far as creation goes.

Lying in wait in circuses and at birthday parties, some people draw the wrong card.

At that point, they may opt to dress up and masquerade as termites in ant farms.

Finally, some people impersonate sheriffs serving eviction notices with or without undue intent to harm.

Marathon Runners

The Yamasee Indians have a habit of running half-way around the continent and back again.

They run for blessings of peace on the inner planes. This occurs before they have solved the liquidation of assets gained from the plantations in the Amazonian forest.

Now in the harbor in France, why should she stand there with the water coursing around her thighs?

How could she claim the mercenary underpinning of the riptide was responsible for what happened?

Everything dear to her had suddenly been taken, save her life.

Pilgrim of Fire

As pilgrims of journeys to the Carmargue, aren't we protected and blessed?

Why pluck out the eyes of death prematurely?

But the local authorities told us something different.

You can't sit on a park bench. Once more, you can't pray standing on the shore.

The living must not keen the dead.

You need to stop praying or be arrested.

No matter what happens, God remains unconcerned.

Why would anyone drown in the knowledge that love itself were something so absurd?

Other Books by Elizabeth Martina Bishop
All books available through Amazon.com

Irish Tinkers

*(Written under pseudonym Martina O'
Fearadhaigh) with photographs by Janine
Wiedel*

The origin of the Irish Tinkers and of
their secret language, shelta, has long been
the subject of fierce controversy amongst
historians. Some say the were forced into
an itinerant existence by the social and
economic upheavals of the 17th century;
others that they are descendants of a pre-
Celtic class of skilled metal workers and others that they are the remnants
of dispossessed nobility. But whatever their origins the Irish Tinkers are
now threatened on all sides. This book is a permanent record of this
curiously resilient people made while there is still time. The moving
photographs together with the transcribed tape-recordings which show the
tinkers' extraordinary eloquence as they talk about their lives, reveal the
anguish of a people in transition; nostalgia for 'the old days' and uncertainty
about the future.

ISBN-10: 0312436270 • ISBN-13: 978-0312436278.

Feathers in the Wind

Feathers in the Wind represents a
compilation of interrelated themes reflected
in indigenous inspired portraits, both lyric
and pastoral. It evidences the author's deep
connection to the mystical aspects of nature
and her continuing dedication to the
traditional craft of poetry.

ISBN-13: 978-1461030874
ISBN-10: 1461030870 • $9.95

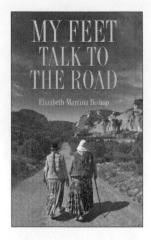

My Feet
Talk to the Road

Traveller culture projects masks involving multiple scenarios. The way of the road may never disappear. The way of the settled folk continues to change. With the disappearance of many itinerant crafts today is born a new integration honoring the old crafts. These days, we can nevertheless appreciate time-honored traditions that invite readers to enter a transcendent dream time. Such an invitation is always present for those who risk a continuous pilgrimage. That is the fearless way of the traveling people.

ISBN-13: 978-1461129646 • ISBN-10: 1461129648 • $14.95

Canary Portals

Canaries have symbolized the healing properties of the sun. Many folk cultures feature the canary as a Rosicrucian dream image showing the canary hovering above a rose. In this narrative poem the canary operates as a fixture, a landmark, leading the dreamer in a journey celebrating life, birth and death.

ISBN-13: 978-1463551179
ISBN-10: 1463551177 • $9.95

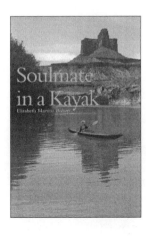

Soulmate in a Kayak

Vignette 1: Soulmate in a Kayak
This section depicts a surreal treatment of a fictitious want ad and the fallout thereof.

Vignette 2: Dervish in a Kiosk
The poems deconstruct the want ad.

Vignette 3: Reinventing Atlantis
Ishti poses questions for those living in so-called civilized society: how can we honor what we don't know we have lost.

Vignette 4: The Green Knight
A pseudo medieval melodrama involving a lovelorn swain who suffers and endures the worst case scenario in a love tryst gone wrong.

ISBN-13: 978-1461154921 • ISBN-10: 1461154928 • $19.95

Leaping into the Unknown

A woman reflects on the meaning of life and turns the sheepfold into a museum, a sunken garden, and a palimpsest of poetry and art.

ISBN-13: 978-1463741334
ISBN-10: 1463741332 • $19.95

Malvinia's Wedding

A folkloric portrait of a woman waiting by various gates for her beloved who may never arrive. The locations depicted in the text are considered in a visionary and fictional manner.

Part dream, part reverie the quilt of stories supports tribal voices heard in the region of Moorish Spain.

ISBN-13: 978-1475161427
ISBN-10: 1475161425
$19.95

The Wedding Will Not Take Place

This poetic novel promises an occasion for celebration and ceremony. Meanwhile, the ritual of ceremony exists only within the mind of the celebrants who are on the point of undertaking a long journey.
This novel promises an ambitious time line involving the completion of a journey. However, no actual ritual of ceremony is actually performed. Instead, the act of writing is seen as a self-redemptive and self-revelatory journey occasioning a spiritual awakening. In the spirit of "Waiting for Godot," celebrants and attendants engage in long journeys of pilgrimage, ultimately leading them towards an inner heart-centered labyrinth. A novel approach to writing a novel without an apparent ending or beginning, words in themselves represent an exploration of the psyches of those who would prepare for a centered afterlife of joy and renunciation.

ISBN-13: 978-1475161205 • ISBN-10: 1475161204 • $18.95

Wind Rushing Through a Nest of Stars

A delectable award-winning study of poetry that will arouse the sleeping palette of connoisseurs.

A wine-tasting array of poetry that shifts our focus to environmental causes. Poems with emotional clout bring us to a deeper sense of awareness. We awake from our sleep with poetry and well crafted poems singing before we take on the day.

ISBN-13: 978-1475182835 • ISBN-10: 147518283X • $14.95

Your Grandmother Knew How To Read Cards

From time immemorial, grandmothers have been in the know about the occult arts. They also know how to read palms. Some of them even write poetry that will make you laugh.

ISBN-13: 978-1479132232
ISBN-10: 1479132233 • $ 9.95

Stonehenge Blues Vol. 1

A mysterious and poignant exploration of poetic memoir to deepen an awareness of who we are and where we are headed. In days of uncertainty we find our footing. We find poetry in an urban coming of age story. How does one interpret life events that seem in old age to have a dream-like quality? In any event it is up to each individual to transmute and transform seemingly meaningless events. Eventually, we find out we are wordsmiths who must take the time to witness hidden worlds. In that way, the art of becoming becomes an art form. We discover who we were all along: pilgrims and solitary seers.

ISBN-13: 978-1479294268 • ISBN-10: 1479294268 • $9.95

Stonehenge Blues Vol. 2

Stonehenge Blues represents the continued journey into the life cycle of birth, marriage, and death. When bohemian-minded poets get together, they have unique ways of summoning forth the wilderness of heart songs. Their world is ever expanding, one which embraces life's teaching moments. That perspective ultimately leads to meditation in the wise solitude of old age. You may want to look at such moments of great passionate intensity with a sense of humorous non-attachment.

ISBN-13: 978-1479294329 • ISBN-10: 1479294322 • $9.95

Carillon Players and Night Watchmen

These poems celebrate an abandoned culture of relationship and an industry based on handcrafts. A cross between the melancholia of a lost way of life and contemporary media driven culture. Between the old world of wandering minstrels, Indian warriors, and a new world in which technology is often the new poetry.

ISBN-13: 978-1480271425 • ISBN-10: 148027142X • $9.95

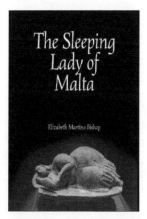

The Sleeping Lady of Malta

An archeological gem, The Sleeping Lady of Malta explores relationship between human, animal and nature and the mystery that no one single poem can evoke.

Native American images predominate because they are cloaked with formidable shadows. This collection offers a credo as to why I write poetry. To experience banner moments of consciousness wherein aesthetics and a love of word smithing is born. The quest for self-knowledge and self-revelation takes nature as its meditation.

ISBN-13: 978-1481946421 • ISBN-10: 1481946420 • $9.95

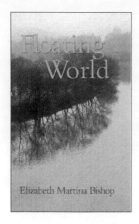

Floating World

Poetic excursions and aesthetic exercises that demonstrate the power of the word. The journey readers take will show them unique pathways through often oblique patterns and designs.

Experimental in nature, these poems push the envelope of time and space and express gratitude for the spiritual.

ISBN-13: 978-1482613186
ISBN-10: 1482613182 • $9.95

And Then I Heard Them Singing

For poets, the culture of every day life involves engagement and interaction implicit in her ongoing conversation. A conversation with creatures of the natural world.

These poems offer whimsical and often comical glimpses into old age, thoughts about the afterlife, and the daily karma of survival.

ISBN-13: 978-1482762853
ISBN-10: 1482762854 • $9.95

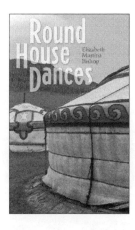

Round House Dances

Round House Dances gifts readers with glimpses into the worlds of the bee shaman, views of the natural world in Ireland and in Boulder, as well as additional encounters with teachers and students.

Everyday experiences surrender readers with poetic vignettes, philosophical, scintillating, meditative, and reflective. A must read for those who seek heart-centered poetry.

ISBN-13: 978-1482763331   •   ISBN-10: 1482763338   • $9.99

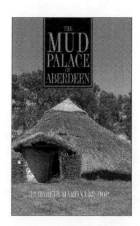

The Mud Palace of Aberdeen

Here are cogent poems that ask questions. Questions that cannot necessarily be answered. Or poetic explorations of parallel worlds. Explorations into unknown and uncharted territory. A whirlwind tour of Native American shamanism. Or just plain shamanism.

The price of being a poet is to create unexplained patchwork quilts in response to the more mysterious aspects of the world around us. Come and enjoy and savor the poetic experience as rich as a good cup of coffee savored in the universal cafe, scintillating, meditative, and reflective.

ISBN-13: 978-1484926918   •   ISBN-10: 1484926919   • $9.95

Beach Side Motel

Life sketches reveal inside stories and inner lives of poets who move from place to place.

Each story, each vignette invites a cosmic awareness of paradise on earth

ISBN-13: 978-1490538716
ISBN-10: 1490538712
$9.95

The Road To Tramore

The Road To Tramore gifts readers with glimpses into visionary worlds, the natural world in Ireland and in Boulder, as well as additional encounters with teachers and students who can unexpectedly appear everywhere.

Everyday experiences surrender readers with poetic vignettes, philosophical, scintillating, meditative, and reflective.

A must read for those who seek heart-centered poetry.

ISBN-13: 978-1490538716
ISBN-10: 1490538712
$17.95

Mistaken Identity

How can you, the reader, awaken to the cosmic dance of poetry?

By savoring the welcome dance of images, visions, and poetic excursions. Can't afford a cruise? Go on cruise control with this poetry and enjoy the ride. These works will sensitize your awareness so you can soon set sail on the vast sea of improvisation. Watch as the stirring of your mind, body, and soul will harmonize with a poet's passion for the caress of words.

ISBN-13: 978-1490956305
ISBN-10: 1490956301
$12.95

Made in the USA
Charleston, SC
09 May 2014